IOWA

HELLO
U.S.A.

by Rita C. LaDoux

Lerner Publications Company

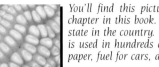

You'll find this picture of kernels of corn at the beginning of each chapter in this book. Iowa farmers produce more corn than any other state in the country. Corn from Iowa is shipped all over the world and is used in hundreds of products—from food for people and animals to paper, fuel for cars, and plastics.

Cover (left): Barn and cornfield in rural Iowa. Cover (right): National Balloon Classic race in Indianola. Pages 2–3: Pier overlooking Spirit Lake. Page 3: Downtown Des Moines.

This book is available in two editions:
Library binding by Lerner Publications Company, a division of Lerner Publishing Group
Soft cover by First Avenue Editions, an imprint of Lerner Publishing Group
241 First Avenue North
Minneapolis, MN 55401 U.S.A.

Website address: www.lernerbooks.com

Library of Congress Cataloging-in-Publication Data

LaDoux, Rita, 1951–
    Iowa / by Rita C. LaDoux. (Rev. and expanded 2nd ed.)
        p.   cm. — (Hello U.S.A.)
    Includes index.
    Summary: An introduction to the land, history, people, economy, and environment of Iowa.
        ISBN: 0–8225–4078–9 (lib. bdg. : alk. paper)
        ISBN: 0–8225–0779–X (pbk. : alk. paper)
        1. Iowa—Juvenile literature. [1. Iowa.] I. Title. II. Series.
    F621.3 .L3 2002
    977.7—dc21   2001006406

Manufactured in the United States of America
1 2 3 4 5 6 – JR – 07 06 05 04 03 02

CONTENTS

Green rolling hills, known as the Loess Hills, cover much of western Iowa.

THE LAND

Rich Prairie Soil

ick up a handful of Iowa's soil—smell it, feel it, look at it—and you will know that the wealth of this state lies in its rich black dirt. About one-fourth of the best farmland in the United States is found in the state of Iowa. The fertile land produces abundant crops of soybeans, hay, and oats, but the state's most famous crop is corn.

A butterfly rests on a zinnia, one of the many flowers that grow in Iowa.

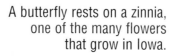

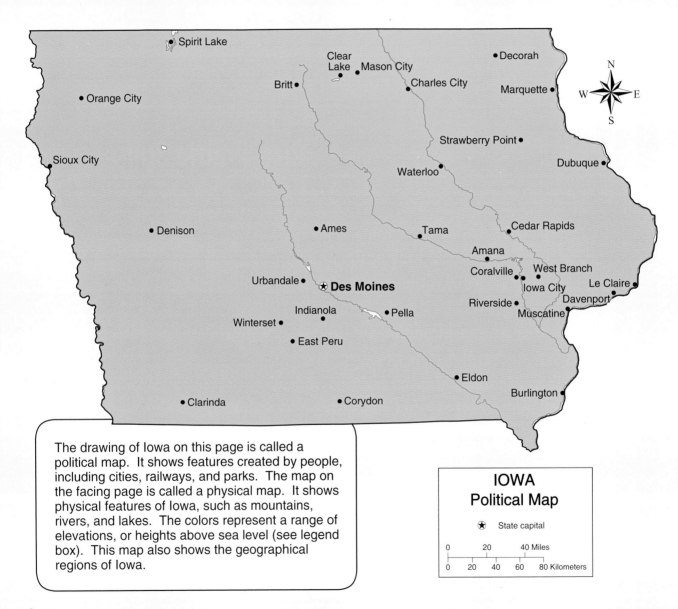

Spirit Lake

Clear Lake

Mason City

Decorah

Britt

Charles City

Marquette

Orange City

Strawberry Point

Dubuque

Sioux City

Waterloo

Denison

Ames

Tama

Cedar Rapids

Amana

Coralville

West Branch

Urbandale

⭐ **Des Moines**

Iowa City

Le Claire

Riverside

Davenport

Indianola

Pella

Muscatine

Winterset

East Peru

Eldon

Burlington

Clarinda

Corydon

The drawing of Iowa on this page is called a political map. It shows features created by people, including cities, railways, and parks. The map on the facing page is called a physical map. It shows physical features of Iowa, such as mountains, rivers, and lakes. The colors represent a range of elevations, or heights above sea level (see legend box). This map also shows the geographical regions of Iowa.

IOWA
Political Map

⭐ State capital

0		20		40 Miles
0	20	40	60	80 Kilometers

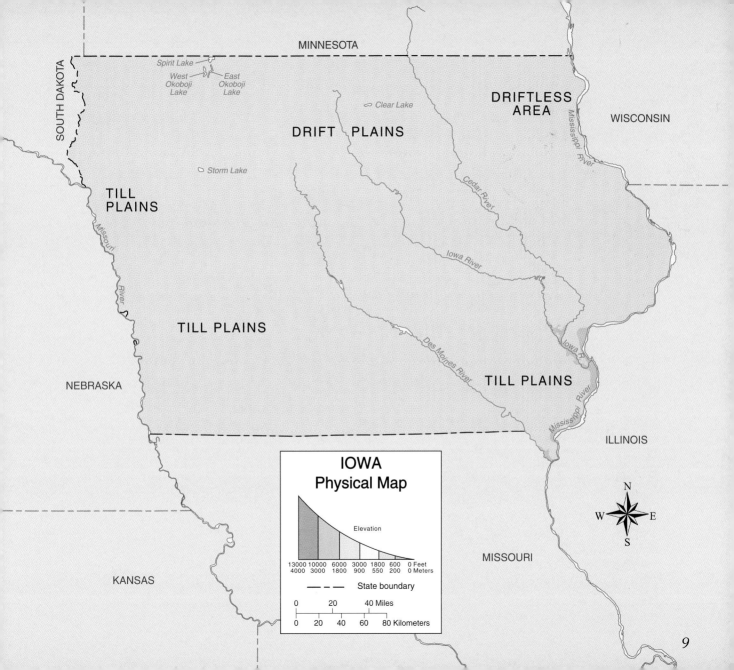

MINNESOTA

SOUTH DAKOTA

Spirit Lake

West
Okoboji
Lake

East
Okoboji
Lake

Clear Lake

DRIFTLESS
AREA

WISCONSIN

DRIFT PLAINS

Storm Lake

Cedar River

TILL
PLAINS

Mississippi River

Missouri River

Iowa River

TILL PLAINS

Des Moines River

NEBRASKA

Iowa R.

TILL PLAINS

Mississippi River

ILLINOIS

IOWA
Physical Map

Elevation

| 13000 | 10000 | 6000 | 3000 | 1800 | 600 | 0 Feet |
| 4000 | 3000 | 1800 | 900 | 550 | 200 | 0 Meters |

- - - State boundary

0   20   40 Miles

0   20   40   60   80 Kilometers

MISSOURI

N
W   E
S

KANSAS

9

Farmland covers much of the Drift Plains region of central Iowa.

Iowa is in the heart of the Midwest. Iowa's eastern neighbors are Wisconsin and Illinois. To the west lie Nebraska and South Dakota. Minnesota borders Iowa on the north, and Missouri is Iowa's southern neighbor.

Iowa has three geographical regions— the Till Plains, the Drift Plains, and the Driftless Area. They were shaped by huge, slow-moving sheets of ice called **glaciers.** The glaciers crept down from the north during the last **ice age,** which began almost 2 million years ago. As the glaciers moved over the land, they flattened hills and crushed boulders and rocks.

Glaciers created Iowa's rich, hilly farmland.

In the southern and western parts of Iowa, glaciers left ground-up boulders and rocks—a mixture known as **till**—on the plains. Streams gradually carved valleys into the till-covered plains. In modern times, farmers raise crops and graze beef cattle on the rich land of this region, called the Till Plains.

Central Iowa holds the state's richest soil. In this region, called the Drift Plains, water from melting glaciers washed more rocky material onto the till. Thick layers of this mixture, called **drift,** were left on the plains. The drift settled unevenly, leaving many small hollows in the land. Water collected in these hollows and created lakes, such as Spirit, East and West Okoboji, Storm, and Clear. Much of Iowa's corn grows on the Drift Plains.

A glacier that crossed the northeastern corner of Iowa covered the area with drift. But wind and water carried away much of it, leaving the region driftless. This Driftless Area is too hilly for farming, but it has good pasture for dairy cattle.

Two major rivers, the Mississippi to the east and the Missouri to the west, create two of Iowa's borders.

Madison County in southern Iowa is famous for its covered bridges.

The Mississippi River forms Iowa's eastern border.

Shorter rivers flow across western Iowa to join the Missouri. Longer rivers—including the Des Moines, Iowa, and Cedar—wind across eastern Iowa and empty into the Mississippi.

Iowa is far enough north to have plenty of snow. Each winter, Iowans may shovel 22 inches or more of snow. Winter temperatures can drop as low as −20° F. Spring and summer winds carry warm, moist air into Iowa, making these seasons fairly rainy. Summers can be very hot. Sometimes the thermometer tops 100° F in July and August.

Iowa's wildflowers include the wild rose *(left)*. Lakes and woodlands dot the landscape *(below)*.

Long before farmers began to raise crops, Iowa was mostly **prairie,** or grassland. Narrow strips of forest shaded the riverbanks. A variety of trees thrive in Iowa, but there are no large forests. Oak, hickory, walnut, and elm trees grow in river valleys. In the Driftless Area, white pine, balsam firs, and cedar trees blanket the hills.

Thousands of buffalo once lived on Iowa's prairies, but only a few still roam in the state. The most common animals in Iowa include white-tailed deer, rabbits, foxes, squirrels, and raccoons. Pheasants, quails, and partridges nest in grain fields. Each year, thousands of ducks and geese fly through Iowa on their way south for the winter and north for the summer.

White-tailed deer make their homes in the Iowa countryside.

Thousands of snow geese arrive on the banks of the Missouri River.

A Changing Landscape

The story of Iowa's people began as the last glaciers melted from the prairies. Indian hunters, the first people in the area, may have come to Iowa as early as 20,000 years ago. They hunted mammoths, huge animals that looked like hairy elephants.

The Indians, also called Native Americans, also gathered seeds, fruits, and nuts to eat. They made clothes from the skin and fur of animals. They lived in caves and in shelters that they could take down and move easily while on a hunt.

Iowa's early people hunted and fished for food.

Mammoths were an important source of food for the early inhabitants of Iowa.

Early Indians made large earthen mounds in the shapes of birds and mammals.

Native Americans lived off the land, gathering nuts, fruits, and seeds.

A new group of Indians came to the eastern part of Iowa in about 300 B.C. These people, called mound builders, built large earthen mounds. The Indians buried their dead in some of these mounds and built temples on top of other mounds.

Iowa's mound builders planted crops such as corn, beans, and squash. No one is sure why, but these Indians disappeared about 500 years ago. Scientists believe that wars, disease, or a long period of crop failure may explain why the mound builders died out.

Around A.D. 1500, a group of Native Americans called the Iowa moved southwest into Iowa. The state takes its name from these Indians. The name probably comes from a word meaning "sleepy ones" in a Native American language.

Iowa takes its name from the Iowa Indians.

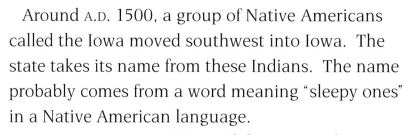

Many of the Iowa Indians farmed and built villages close to the banks of the Mississippi River. Others moved west to the Missouri River. Those who went west eventually split into two tribes—the Missouri and the Oto.

The Iowa, Oto, and Missouri peoples lived in earthen lodges, which they built along the wooded river valleys. In spring the Indians planted crops such as corn, beans, squash, and tobacco. When summer came, men left their villages to hunt buffalo on the prairies.

Many other Indian groups hunted on Iowa's prairies. These groups included the Sauk and the Fox, who lived east of the Mississippi River, and the Omaha and the Osage, who lived close to the Missouri River. In fall the hunters returned to their villages to harvest crops and to make buffalo hides into clothing and other useful objects.

The Sauk and the Fox Indians lived east of the Mississippi River.

With Indians to guide them, Marquette and Jolliet explored the Mississippi River.

The first Europeans to visit Iowa were the French explorers Jacques Marquette and Louis Jolliet. In May 1673, they set out from northern Michigan to explore the Mississippi River. One month later, they pulled their canoes onto the Mississippi's riverbanks in northern Iowa.

Nine years later, in 1682, explorer Sieur de la Salle traveled down the Mississippi River. He claimed the entire Mississippi River valley, including Iowa, for France. La Salle named the land Louisiana, after Louis XIV, the king of France.

During the 1700s, very few white people visited the area that became Iowa. In 1788 the Fox Indians gave permission to French-Canadian pioneer Julien Dubuque to mine lead on their land near the present-day city of Dubuque. Julien Dubuque was Iowa's first white settler.

The city of Dubuque is named for Julien Dubuque.

Black Hawk and his followers were defeated by U.S. soldiers.

The region became part of the United States in 1803, when France sold Louisiana to the United States. During the Black Hawk War of 1832, U.S. government troops defeated Indian warriors led by Chief Black Hawk, a Sauk leader. After their defeat, Sauk and Fox Indians were forced off a strip of land along the Mississippi River in Iowa.

Afterward, many white settlers began to come to eastern Iowa. As settlers gradually pushed farther into Iowa, the U.S. government forced Indians to sell their land and move west onto **reservations**—areas of land set aside for Native Americans. Between 1824 and 1851, Native Americans lost all their land in Iowa.

Iowa's rich farmland attracted men and women from Ohio, Indiana, Illinois, Wisconsin, and Michigan. Later, people arrived from Germany, Great Britain, Norway, and the Netherlands.

Visitors can learn about life on early Iowa farms at living history villages.

Irish miners came to work in the lead mines near Dubuque.

In 1838 Iowa became a territory of the United States. This meant that residents had to follow U.S. laws, but they had fewer rights than people living in states. The Territory of Iowa included present-day Iowa, most of present-day Minnesota, and parts of North and South Dakota.

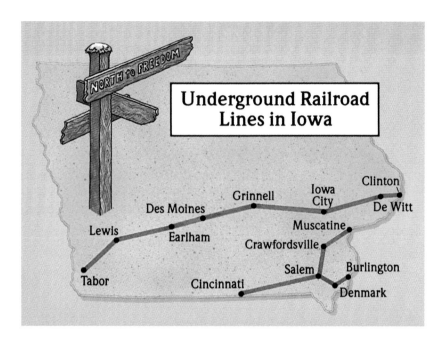

Underground Railroad Lines in Iowa

NORTH to FREEDOM

Clinton
De Witt
Iowa City
Grinnell
Des Moines
Muscatine
Lewis
Earlham
Crawfordsville
Salem
Burlington
Tabor
Cincinnati
Denmark

Slaves escaping north to Canada used a secret network called the Underground Railroad. The "railroad" ran through Iowa and other states that didn't allow slavery. Many Iowans helped the slaves as they traveled.

In the 1840s, the territory's residents argued about whether or not Iowa should become a state. Many people were against statehood. They didn't want to pay taxes to pay the salaries of local leaders. Other people favored statehood but couldn't agree on what the state's boundaries should be.

In the mid-1800s, tension was building in the United States over the issue of slavery. Many people in Southern states used slave labor, and slavery was legal in the South. But in the North, slavery was illegal.

To avoid conflict between the North and the South, the U.S. government tried to keep the number of Southern slave states equal to the number of Northern free states. Iowans were ready for statehood at the same time people in Florida were, so the U.S. government paired Iowa, a free state, with Florida, a slave state. On December 28, 1846, Iowa became the 29th state in the United States.

The argument over slavery led to the Civil War—the war between the North and the South. The war began in 1861, and Iowa's men joined the Northern forces. No battles were fought in the state, but more than 12,500 of Iowa's soldiers died. Women in Iowa ran family farms during the war and served the troops as nurses.

An engraving from William Still's book *The Underground Railroad* shows fugitive African American slaves shooting slave catchers who pursue them as they escape in a covered wagon.

D. V.

DVRR

Railroads allowed farmers to ship their crops to far-off cities.

The North won the war in 1865. Afterward, Iowans went to work planting crops and building farms and roads. To encourage railroad owners to build tracks in Iowa, the government gave more than one-tenth of the state's land to railroad companies. Trains brought more people to Iowa and enabled Iowa's farmers to ship their crops quickly to markets in many U.S. cities.

But the railroads charged farmers very high prices to ship their products. The farmers thought these prices were unfair. To fight the railroad companies, many farmers joined the Grange, a national farmers' group organized in 1867. More people joined the Grange in Iowa than in any other state. In 1874 the first of Iowa's Granger laws was passed. These laws required the railroad companies and the state government to work together to set fair prices.

This picture from 1880 shows lumber being floated down the Mississippi River.

The Right to Vote

Carrie Chapman Catt was born in Wisconsin in 1859. She grew up near Charles City, Iowa. After high school, her father said she couldn't go to college, but that didn't stop her. She earned enough money to pay for classes at Iowa State College in Ames. By 1883 she supervised all the schools in Mason City, Iowa.

At that time, it was unusual for a woman to have such an important job. Women weren't even allowed to vote. But Catt thought that women were smart enough to make decisions for themselves. She began to work for the woman suffrage movement— the struggle to give women the right to vote.

In 1892 Catt moved to New York City, where she joined the National American Woman Suffrage Association. She was so good at organizing groups and coming up with ideas that in 1900 she was chosen to be president of the association.

Catt traveled around the country and was known for her brilliant speeches. To help convince politicians that women should be allowed to vote, she spoke before the U.S. Congress. The hard work finally paid off. In 1920 the 19th Amendment, giving women the right to vote in all U.S. elections, was added to the U.S. Constitution.

During World War I (1914–1918), people in war-torn Europe needed food from the United States. Iowa's farmers became rich selling corn for high prices. To make even more money, many of Iowa's farmers borrowed money from banks to buy bigger farms. Then, after the war, crop prices fell. Farmers found it hard to pay back their bank loans.

During World War I, Iowa's corn crop was in high demand.

The Buxton Community

In 1900 a small coal-mining town called Buxton was built in southeastern Iowa. By 1910 Buxton had about 6,000 residents, more than half of them African Americans. Some of Buxton's black citizens had jobs as coal miners, but many others worked as doctors, dentists, lawyers, accountants, teachers, and school principals.

At a time when many public places in the United States were segregated—or separated—by race, the black people and white people of Buxton worked and lived side by side. They ate at restaurants together, went to school together, and drank from the same water fountains.

Buxton didn't last long, though. When the nearby coal mine closed, Buxton's residents left to find jobs in bigger cities. Many African Americans weren't able to find good jobs like they'd had in Buxton. The town of Buxton was abandoned by 1925, but its residents never forgot this early example of equality between black people and white people.

The Great Depression soon followed. Banks failed, factories and businesses closed, and workers lost their jobs. In Iowa many farms failed, and farmers lost their land.

In the early 1930s, President Franklin D. Roosevelt started the New Deal, a plan to help the nation recover from the depression. New Deal projects helped Iowa's farmers pay back bank loans and buy new equipment. One New Deal program brought electricity to rural areas, improving life for many Iowans.

The government helped Iowa farmers build electric power lines in the 1930s.

Companies such as Pioneer developed improved kinds of corn and other crops.

In 1939 World War II broke out in Europe. During the war, most of Iowa's farmers began to plant a new kind of corn. Called hybrid corn, this corn had large, high-quality ears. Hybrid corn grew so well that farmers were able to grow more corn than ever before. Iowa's farmers began to make money again because they could sell corn and other crops in Europe for high prices.

By the time the war ended, in 1945, many new food-processing and manufacturing plants had come to Iowa's cities. On the farms, people used modern machinery to do the heavy work. Farms needed fewer workers. People began to leave Iowa's rural areas to find jobs in new factories in the cities. By the 1960s, more Iowans lived in cities than in small towns or on farms.

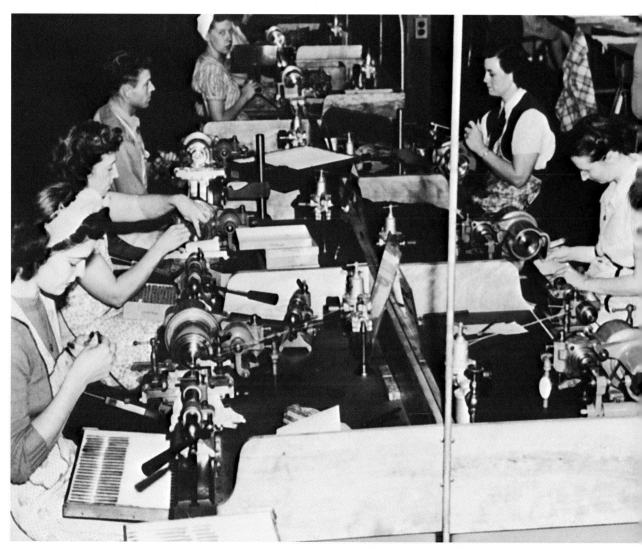

In the 1940s, many Iowans left their farms to take jobs in factories and processing plants.

During the 1970s, manufacturing was earning more money for the state than agriculture was. Crop prices crashed in the 1980s, causing more farmers to leave their land. Many young Iowans decided to leave the state to look for better jobs.

In 1989 the state government legalized riverboat gambling in Iowa. Riverboat casinos began operating in 1991. The casinos are located on old-fashioned riverboats, just like the ones that traveled on the Mississippi River in the 1800s. People can enjoy gambling, food, and entertainment at the casinos. Riverboat gambling has attracted more tourists to Iowa and created new jobs for Iowa residents.

Several times in the 1990s, flooding caused hardship in Iowa. Heavy rains caused many rivers, including the Mississippi and Missouri, to overflow their banks. In 1993 severe flooding damaged billions of dollars worth of crops, buildings, and other property. That year President Bill Clinton declared the entire state of Iowa a disaster area. The federal government set up programs to help

Iowa's state capitol building in Des Moines has four copper-covered domes and one gold-covered dome.

people who had lost their homes and property during the flood.

Iowa has recovered from the disastrous floods, but the state still faces many challenges. In the years ahead, Iowans hope to keep their farms and businesses strong and to welcome new kinds of businesses to their state.

PEOPLE & ECONOMY

The Heart of the Midwest

Iowa's rich and varied landscape provides both recreation and livelihoods for its residents.

Iowans are proud of their farming heritage. Most of Iowa's nearly 3 million people have roots on the family farm, although many Iowans live in cities. Iowa's largest cities include Des Moines—the state capital—Cedar Rapids, Davenport, Sioux City, Waterloo, and Iowa City.

Almost all Iowans were born in the United States, and most—about 92 percent—have European ancestors. Small numbers of Iowans have African, Latino, Asian, or Native American

Many Iowans celebrate
their Indian heritage
at powwows.

ancestry. About 700
Mesquakie (Fox) and Sauk
Indians live on a settlement
in Tama.

Iowans celebrate their diverse
ethnic heritage at festivals
throughout the state. Native
American culture is highlighted
each year at the Mesquakie
Indian Powwow in Tama.
Many people dance to German
polka bands at Davenport's
Oktoberfest. Nordic Fest in Decorah features
colorful Norwegian costumes and lively dancing.

Iowans take great pride in winning events at the state fair each year.

Each year hundreds of thousands of people gather in Des Moines for another popular event, the Iowa State Fair. Manufacturers display the latest farm machines, and farmers show off their best crops and animals. Many people go to the fair to ride roller coasters or hear performances by famous musicians.

At the Tulip Festival in Orange City, Iowans of Dutch heritage celebrate with traditional costumes, foods, and music.

43

The Bix Beiderbecke Memorial Jazz Festival, held each July in Davenport, attracts thousands of music lovers. Rock music fans gather in Clear Lake each February for the Winter Dance Party. For people who prefer classical music, Davenport offers the Quad City Mozart Festival in summer.

Many of Iowa's small towns host parades and special events. Each May, residents of Orange City and Pella show off their gardening skills at tulip festivals. In June, residents of Corydon act out bank robberies staged by Jesse James and his gang in the 1800s. People in Strawberry Point enjoy strawberries and ice cream as part of their celebration of Strawberry Days each June.

Iowans also enjoy preserving and learning about their history. Effigy Mounds National Monument near Marquette features the ancient burial mounds of Iowa's mound builders. Tourists at the Living History Farms in

Indianola holds its National Hot Air Balloon Classic every August.

Des Moines can visit a farm like the one their pioneer ancestors might have lived on. West Branch's Herbert Hoover National Historic Site displays the cottage where President Herbert Hoover was born in 1874.

Sports fans throughout the state cheer on their favorite high school and college teams. Wrestling, basketball, track, and softball are popular sports. Nearly everyone chooses sides when the Cyclones from Iowa State University meet the Hawkeyes of the University of Iowa on the football field.

The rivalry between the Iowa State Cyclones and the University of Iowa Hawkeyes football teams has raged for years.

Bicycling, golf, hiking, and camping are also popular activities. In the summer, vacationers relax at the lakes near the town of Spirit Lake in northern Iowa. In the winter, cross-country skiers glide along snow-covered trails.

Iowa's woodlands offer peaceful spots for recreation year-round.

Des Moines is home to many insurance companies.

About 60 percent of the state's workers have service jobs, helping people or businesses. Salespeople, doctors, mechanics, bankers, and insurance agents are all service workers. More than 50 insurance companies have their main offices in Des Moines. These companies help pay for damages to people and property.

Behind the scenes at a Sioux City popcorn plant *(left)*. Food processing is an important Iowa industry *(below)*.

Manufacturing is another important industry in Iowa. Many people make breakfast sausage or can hams in large meatpacking plants. Some Iowans process corn into products such as corn oil and cornstarch. Workers in Sioux City process popcorn. Other Iowans make dairy products. At plants in Davenport, Des Moines, Dubuque, and Waterloo, workers build farm machinery.

About 8 percent of Iowans work on farms, and more than 90 percent of Iowa's land is farmland. Iowa leads all states in corn production and ranks among the top states in soybean production. Hay, oats, and alfalfa are also important crops in the state.

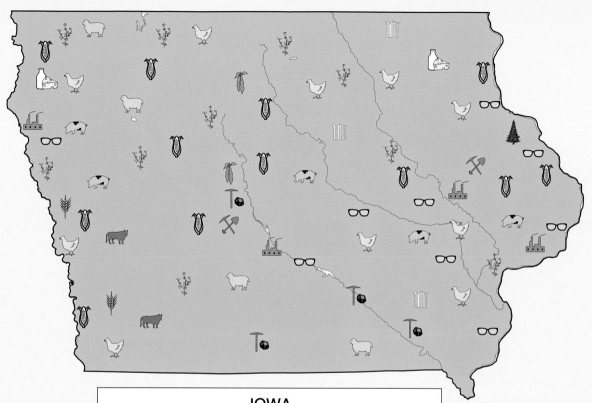

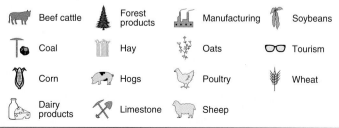

IOWA
Economic Map

The symbols on this map show where different economic activities take place in Iowa. The legend below explains what each symbol stands for.

Symbol	Activity	Symbol	Activity	Symbol	Activity	Symbol	Activity
	Beef cattle		Forest products		Manufacturing		Soybeans
	Coal		Hay		Oats		Tourism
	Corn		Hogs		Poultry		Wheat
	Dairy products		Limestone		Sheep		

Farmers in Iowa raise more hogs than farmers in any other state. Other animals raised in Iowa include beef and dairy cattle, turkeys, and chickens. Iowa's farmers also harvest bushels of apples. The red Delicious apple was developed at an orchard near East Peru, Iowa, in the 1880s. The red Delicious is still one of the most popular apples in the United States.

Some Iowans make their living by digging limestone, sand, gravel, clay, or gypsum. These minerals are used to make cement and other construction materials. Miners dig coal in central and southern Iowa. Power plants burn coal to generate most of Iowa's electricity.

From farmers to bankers to salesclerks, Iowans depend on the rich soil of their state. Farmers sell their crops and livestock to manufacturers. Farm earnings are held in banks. Manufacturers and store owners count on farmers to buy equipment, fertilizers, and clothes. In this way, the state's land provides jobs for many people.

Some Iowans make a living by raising crops and livestock.

THE ENVIRONMENT

Striking a Healthy Balance

Rich soil and the promise of abundant crops brought many pioneer farmers to Iowa. Corn grew so well in the state that farmers planted more and more of it. By 1880 Iowa's farmers had planted most of their land with corn. But problems such as weeds and insects eventually began to plague Iowa's farms.

Some plants use up nutrients, or food, in the soil. For instance, corn takes nitrogen from the soil. Nitrogen is an important nutrient for plants. When Iowa's farmers planted their fields with nothing but corn, nitrogen levels fell. In time, the corn did not grow as well.

Iowa's main environmental challenge is finding a balance between growing healthy crops and keeping the soil and water pollution-free.

A plane sprays insecticide on a cornfield *(above)* in an effort to keep insects from destroying corn *(right).*

To produce more corn, Iowa's farmers spread chemical **fertilizers** on their fields. They also sprayed fields with **herbicides** to kill weeds and **insecticides** to kill insects. But fertilizers, herbicides, and insecticides can harm people, plants, and animals. These chemicals often run off from farms into rivers and lakes. They poison the plants and animals that live in and around the water. Chemicals sometimes filter down into **groundwater**—the water beneath the earth's surface—poisoning the water that people drink.

A lake has been covered by algae, the result of too much fertilizer used on nearby fields.

Farmers must try to grow healthy crops while also protecting the environment.

Because fertilizers, herbicides, and insecticides can be harmful, some of Iowa's farmers are trying to use fewer chemicals. **Crop rotation** is one way to use less fertilizer. For example, one year a farmer may plant a field of corn, which robs the soil of nitrogen. But the next year, the farmer will plant soybeans, alfalfa, or clover, which put nitrogen back into the soil. Rotating crops in this way helps keep the soil rich, without chemical fertilizers. Rotating crops also helps stop the spread of insects that feed on only one type of crop.

Soybeans help restore nitrogen to the soil.

Iowa has some of the richest soil on earth.

Iowa's farmers have also learned to kill weeds without using any chemicals at all. For instance, by turning over the soil between rows of corn, farmers can tear up weeds the same way a gardener with a hoe does. Farmers are working with scientists and the government to find other ways to grow crops without hurting the land, plants, or animals. People in Iowa want to make sure that their state's rich land will continue to produce bountiful healthy crops for their children and grandchildren.

ALL ABOUT IOWA

Fun Facts

Snake Alley, a street on a hillside in Burlington, Iowa, winds back and forth seven times in 275 feet. Every May top cyclists from around the country compete in the Snake Alley Criterium—a bike race up the steep cobblestone street.

William Morrison of Des Moines, Iowa, built the first successful electric car in the United States. On September 4, 1890, Morrison demonstrated his car. It sat 12 passengers and traveled at an amazing speed of 20 miles per hour!

The Hobo King and Queen are crowned each August at the National Hobo Convention in Britt, Iowa. Hoboes are people who travel from place to place, often hopping onto railroad boxcars to ride across the country. They have gathered in Britt every year since 1900.

Sioux City, Iowa, processes more popcorn than any other city in the United States. Each year workers package tons of popcorn and ship it throughout the world.

Captain Kirk, a character from the television show *Star Trek,* was born in Riverside, Iowa—or so the residents of the town claim. A book about *Star Trek* states that the fictional James T. Kirk was born in a small town in Iowa. The people in Riverside decided it was their town. Every March since 1985, they have thrown a birthday party for Captain Kirk.

Bicycle riders race up Snake Alley every May.

STATE SONG

The words to Iowa's official state song were written in 1897. The song borrows the tune of the traditional German Christmas carol "O Tannenbaum," as do the state songs of Maryland, New Jersey, and Michigan.

THE SONG OF IOWA

Words by Samuel Hawkins Marshall Byers; music traditional

You can hear "The Song of Iowa" by visiting this website:
<http://www.50states.com/songs/iowa.htm>

AN IOWA RECIPE

Red Delicious apples were developed in East Peru, Iowa, in the 1880s. Use red Delicious apples to make tasty caramel apples on a stick.

CARAMEL APPLES

6 red Delicious apples
6 craft sticks
1 14-ounce package of individually wrapped caramels
2 tablespoons milk

1. Butter a baking sheet.
2. Remove the stem from each apple and press a craft stick into the top.
3. Unwrap the caramels. Place them with the milk in a microwave-safe bowl.
4. Microwave for two minutes, stirring once.
5. Allow the caramel sauce to cool briefly.
6. Roll each apple quickly in the caramel sauce until well coated.
7. Place on the baking sheet to set.
8. Refrigerate for about 15 minutes to firm up caramel.

Serves 6.

HISTORICAL TIMELINE

18,000 B.C. Indian hunters follow mammoths into what later became Iowa.

300 B.C. Mound builders arrive in Iowa.

A.D. 1500 Iowa Indians settle in Iowa.

1673 Marquette and Jolliet explore Iowa.

1682 Sieur de la Salle claims Iowa and the entire Mississippi River valley for France.

1788 Julien Dubuque mines lead near Dubuque.

1803 The United States acquires Iowa as part of the Louisiana Purchase.

1808 Fort Madison, the U.S. Army's first fort on the upper Mississippi River, is built in the southeast corner of Iowa.

1832 The U.S. Army defeats the Sauk Indians in the Black Hawk War.

1838 Iowa becomes a U.S. territory.

1846 Iowa becomes the 29th state.

1857   Des Moines becomes the capital of Iowa.

1867   The first railroad across Iowa is completed.

1907   Fred Maytag begins manufacturing washing machines in Iowa.

1913   The Keokuk Dam, the world's largest hydroelectric power plant at the time, goes into operation along the Mississippi River.

1935   The U.S. government helps bring electricity to rural areas in Iowa.

1970s   Manufacturing replaces agriculture as the main source of income for Iowa's residents.

1980s   Many Iowans leave the state to look for better jobs.

1993   Floods cause more than $2 billion in damage to Iowa farms and property.

1996   Iowa celebrates 150 years of statehood.

1997   Bobbi and Kenny McCaughey of Carlisle, Iowa, become the parents of septuplets (seven babies born to one mother at one time).

2000   The University of Iowa wrestling team wins its sixth straight National Collegiate Athletic Association (NCAA) championship.

OUTSTANDING IOWANS

Bill Bryson

Johnny Carson

Roger Craig

Lee De Forest

Bix Beiderbecke (1903–1931), born in Davenport, played with a number of famous 1920s jazz bands, including the Wolverines. Known primarily as a cornet player, Beiderbecke was also a talented pianist, composer, and bandleader.

Bill Bryson (born 1951) is well known for his essays, travel books, and books about the history of the English language. Bryson was born in Des Moines but lived in England for almost 20 years.

Johnny Carson (born 1925) was born in Corning, Iowa, but grew up in Nebraska. He began his career as a radio announcer and then moved on to television. Known for his quick wit, Carson hosted *The Tonight Show* from 1962 to 1992.

Buffalo Bill Cody (1846–1917) was born William Frederick Cody in Le Claire, Iowa. A frontiersman and noted marksman, Cody opened Buffalo Bill's Wild West show in 1883. The show toured the United States and parts of Europe. It featured mock Indian battles and shooting demonstrations.

Roger Craig (born 1960) is from Davenport, Iowa. As a running back for the San Francisco 49ers, Craig led his team in rushing from 1985 to 1989. He set an NFL record in 1985, when he gained 1,000 yards receiving and 1,000 yards rushing in a single season. Craig retired from professional football in 1994.

Lee De Forest (1873–1961) began inventing as a boy in Council Bluffs, Iowa. Called the Father of Radio, De Forest received patents for hundreds of inventions, including the audion tube, a device for sending radio waves without wires.

Bob Feller (born 1918) was born in Van Meter, Iowa. He was a pitcher with the Cleveland Indians baseball team for 18 years. During his career, he pitched three no-hitters and led the American League in strikeouts seven times. In 1962 he was elected to the Baseball Hall of Fame.

Bob Feller

George Gallup (1901–1984) came from Jefferson, Iowa. He developed the Gallup Poll, a survey of public opinion on many issues. The first major success of the Gallup Poll came in 1936, when the poll correctly predicted that Franklin D. Roosevelt would be elected president.

Janet Guthrie

Janet Guthrie (born 1938), from Iowa City, gave up a career as an aerospace physicist to concentrate on auto racing. In 1977 she became the first woman to drive in the Indianapolis 500. Although her engine failed that year and she could not finish, Guthrie returned in 1978 to become the first woman to complete the race.

Halston

Halston (1932–1990), born in Des Moines, operated his fashion business from New York City. He started his career by designing hats. He branched into clothing design in 1966. In 1974 Halston was named to the Coty Hall of Fame.

Herbert Hoover (1874–1964) was born in West Branch, Iowa. He became a successful engineer and businessman and held a number of political offices, including U.S. secretary of commerce. Hoover served as the 31st president of the United States from 1929 to 1933, during the early years of the Great Depression.

Herbert Hoover

John L. Lewis

Glenn Miller

Harry Reasoner

Donna Reed

Ann Landers (Esther Lederer) and **Abigail Van Buren** (Pauline Phillips) were born on July 4, 1918, in Sioux City, Iowa. The identical twin sisters have written separate advice columns for almost 50 years.

John L. Lewis (1880–1964) was born near Lucas, Iowa. After completing seventh grade, he left school to work in a coal mine. In 1935 he founded the Committee for Industrial Organization (later the Congress of Industrial Organizations), a powerful group of labor unions. Lewis served as president of the United Mine Workers of America from 1920 to 1960.

Frederick Maytag (1857–1937) grew up in Newton, Iowa. Maytag manufactured farm machinery for many years before he started making and selling washing machines in 1907. By 1925 Maytag's company was the biggest washing machine manufacturer in the world.

Glenn Miller (1904–1944) was born in Clarinda, Iowa. He led the famous Glenn Miller Orchestra, a dance band, during the late 1930s and early 1940s. Miller and his band recorded many hit songs, including "Moonlight Serenade," "Chattanooga Choo Choo," and "Kalamazoo."

Harry Reasoner (1923–1991), a native of Dakota City, Iowa, worked in national television news for 35 years. He was a reporter, news correspondent, and anchor for CBS and ABC.

Donna Reed (1921–1986) was born in Denison, Iowa. She appeared in the movie *It's a Wonderful Life* with Jimmy Stewart in 1946. In 1953 she won an Academy Award for her role in *From Here to Eternity.* She starred in *The Donna Reed Show,* a TV situation comedy, from 1958 to 1966.

Charles Ringling (1863–1926), born in McGregor, Iowa, formed a little circus with four of his brothers in 1884. At first they traveled by wagon with two animal performers—a trained horse and a dancing bear. By 1907 the Ringling Brothers had the largest circus in the world.

Charles Ringling

Jacob Schick (1877–1937), a Des Moines native, invented the electric razor. He sold more than 1.8 million razors between 1931 and his death in 1937.

Wallace Stegner (1909–1993), a native of Lake Mills, Iowa, wrote novels, biographies, and essays celebrating the American West. Stegner's best-known works include *The Big Rock Candy Mountain*, *Crossing to Safety*, and *Angle of Repose*, for which he won the Pulitzer Prize for literature.

Jacob Schick

Billy Sunday (1862–1935), born in Ames, was a professional baseball player and evangelist. His baseball career with the Chicago White Stockings and Pittsburgh Pirates ended when he was called to religious service. Sunday was ordained a minister in the Presbyterian Church in 1903 and began touring the United States spreading his religious message.

John Wayne

John Wayne (1907–1979), a hero of many Western films and war dramas, was born in Winterset, Iowa. He acted in more than 150 films and won an Academy Award for his performance in the 1969 movie *True Grit*.

Grant Wood (1892–1942) was born near Anamosa, Iowa. Because his high school offered no art classes, Wood pursued art training on his own. He became famous for his paintings of life in the Midwest. His best-known work is *American Gothic*.

Grant Wood

FACTS-AT-A-GLANCE

Nickname: Hawkeye State

Song: "The Song of Iowa"

Motto: Our Liberties We Prize and Our Rights We Will Maintain

Flower: wild rose

Tree: oak

Bird: eastern goldfinch

Rock: geode

Fossil (proposed): crinoid

Soil (unofficial): tama

Date and ranking of statehood: December 28, 1846, the 29th state

Capital: Des Moines

Area: 55,875 square miles

Rank in area, nationwide: 23rd

Average July temperature: 75° F

Average January temperature: 19° F

The Iowa flag, adopted in 1921, consists of three vertical stripes of blue, white, and red—the colors of both the French and American flags. The white center stripe displays an eagle holding blue streamers in its beak. The streamers are inscribed with the state's motto.

POPULATION GROWTH

Millions

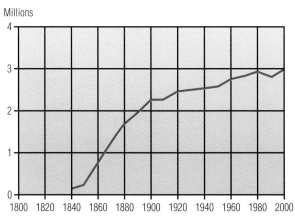

This chart shows how Iowa's population has grown from 1840 to 2000.

Iowa's state seal shows a soldier with an American flag in one hand and a gun in the other. The seal also displays a plow, a sheaf of wheat, and a sickle—representing Iowa's agricultural heritage. A lead furnace (representing manufacturing), the Mississippi River, and an eagle holding the state motto are also pictured on the seal.

Population: 2,926,324 (2000 census)

Rank in population, nationwide: 30th

Major cities and populations: (2000 census) Des Moines (198,682), Cedar Rapids (120,758), Davenport (98,359), Sioux City (85,013), Waterloo (68,747)

U.S. senators: 2

U.S. representatives: 5

Electoral votes: 7

Natural resources: clay, coal, gravel, gypsum, limestone, sand, shale, soil, water

Agricultural products: alfalfa, apples, beef cattle, corn, flaxseed, hay, hogs, milk, oats, poultry, rye, sheep, soybeans, wheat

Manufactured goods: chemicals, electrical equipment, farm machinery, food products, printed materials, metal products

WHERE IOWANS WORK

Services—60 percent (services includes jobs in trade; community, social, and personal services; finance, insurance and real estate; transportation, communication, and utilities)

Manufacturing—14 percent

Government—13 percent

Agriculture—8 percent

Construction—5 percent

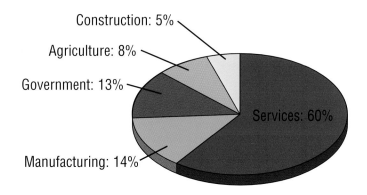

Construction: 5%
Agriculture: 8%
Government: 13%
Services: 60%
Manufacturing: 14%

GROSS STATE PRODUCT

Services—52 percent

Manufacturing—23 percent

Government—11 percent

Agriculture—10 percent

Construction—4 percent

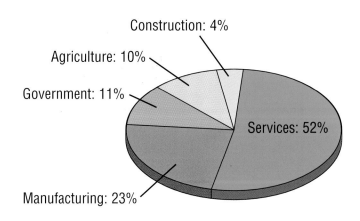

Construction: 4%
Agriculture: 10%
Government: 11%
Services: 52%
Manufacturing: 23%

IOWAN WILDLIFE

Mammals: cottontail rabbit, coyote, fox, jackrabbit, opossum, white-tailed deer

Birds: Canada goose, duck, partridge, quail, ring-necked pheasant

Amphibians and reptiles: frogs, lizards, toads, turtles, salamanders, snakes

Fish: bluegill, catfish, crappie, largemouth bass, northern pike, smallmouth bass, trout, walleye

Trees: balsam fir, cottonwood, elm, hickory, maple, oak, walnut, white pine, willow

Wild plants: bloodroot, gentian, goldenrod, marsh marigold, pasqueflower, prairie aster, prairie lily, purple phlox, sunflower, violet, wild rose

Jackrabbit

PLACES TO VISIT

Amana Colonies, near Cedar Rapids

Amana was a communal society established by German settlers shortly before the Civil War. The site contains 31 historic structures that illustrate the story of the society.

American Gothic House, Eldon

Listed on the National Register of Historic Places, this small white house is pictured in Grant Wood's classic painting *American Gothic*. The house is not open to the public, but visitors can pose like the farm couple in the painting for photographs.

Buffalo Bill Museum, Le Claire

This museum displays Buffalo Bill memorabilia, along with riverboat, steamboat, Indian, and pioneer artifacts.

Crystal Lake Cave, Dubuque

Here visitors can take a guided tour through more than 3,000 feet of lighted passageways and view intricate crystal formations.

Devonian Fossil Gorge, Coralville

The floods of 1993 exposed bedrock deposits from the Devonian Period at this site on Coralville Lake. Visitors can observe fossilized shells and skeletons of sea-dwelling animals that lived about 375 million years ago.

Effigy Mounds National Monument, near Marquette
The monument contains 195 earthen mounds created by Native Americans as early as 300 B.C. Many mounds were built in the shape of mammals, birds, and reptiles.

Herbert Hoover's National Historic Site, West Branch
Visitors can see the small cottage where Herbert Hoover was born in 1874, the first West Branch schoolhouse, the Friends meetinghouse where the Hoover family worshipped, Hoover's grave, and other historic sites and structures.

Iowa State Capitol, Des Moines
Built between 1871 and 1886, this beautiful building contains a variety of marble, artwork, and wood and stone carvings. The main capitol dome is covered with 23-karat gold leaf.

Living History Farms, Urbandale
This 600-acre outdoor museum presents information on five historical time periods spanning 300 years. Sites include the 1700 Ioway Indian Village, the 1850 Pioneer Farm, the 1875 town of Walnut Hill, and the 1900 Farm.

Mississippi River Museum, Dubuque
Visitors can learn about explorers, riverboat pilots, and gamblers through life-sized exhibits covering 300 years of Mississippi River history.

ANNUAL EVENTS

Winter Dance Party, Clear Lake—*February*

Pella Tulip Time, Pella—*May*

Snake Alley Criterium, Burlington—*May*

Glenn Miller Festival, Clarinda—*June*

Grant Wood Art Festival, Stone City—*June*

TrekFest, Riverside—*June*

Bix Beiderbecke Festival, Davenport—*July*

Register's Annual Great Bicycle Ride Across Iowa (RAGBRAI), Sioux City to Muscatine—*July*

Hobo Festival, Britt—*August*

Mesquakie Indian Powwow, Tama—*August*

National Hot Air Balloon Classic, Indianola—*August*

Madison Covered Bridge Festival, Winterset—*October*

It's a Wonderful Life Festival, Denison—*December*

LEARN MORE ABOUT IOWA

BOOKS

General

Fradin, Dennis Brindell. *Iowa.* Chicago: Children's Press, 1995.

Hintz, Martin. *Iowa.* Danbury, CT: Children's Press, 2000. For older readers.

Morrice, Polly. *Iowa.* Tarrytown, NY: Marshall Cavendish Inc., 1998. For older readers.

Special Interest

Artley, Bob. *Once upon a Farm.* Gretna, LA: Pelican Publishing, 2000. Author and illustrator Bob Artley looks back at farm life in the early 1900s by recalling his own Iowa childhood. The book includes Artley's recollections as well as his water-color paintings and sketches.

Collins, David R. *Bix Beiderbecke: Jazz Age Genius.* Greensboro, NC: Morgan Reynolds, 1998. Iowa-born Beiderbecke was a gifted cornet player, pianist, and composer. As a bandleader, he helped usher in the Jazz Age of the 1920s. For older readers.

Duggleby, John. *Artist in Overalls: The Life of Grant Wood.* San Francisco: Chronicle Books, 1996. This biography details the life and work of Wood, most famous for his classic painting *American Gothic.*

Johnson, Rebecca. *A Walk in the Prairie.* Minneapolis: Carolrhoda Books, Inc., 2000. This book introduces readers to the prairie ecosystem, the biological community that covered most of Iowa before the days of farming.

Fiction

Lawlor, Laurie. *Addie's Forever Friend.* Morton Grove, IL: Albert Whitman & Co., 1997. Set in Iowa in the 1880s, this book tells about farm girl Addie and her friends, family, and hopes for the future.

Speerstra, Karen. *The Earthshapers.* Happy Camp, CA: Naturegraph, 1992. This story follows fictional Yellow Moon, a 12-year-old mound builder girl living around A.D. 900 in the northern Mississippi Valley around present-day Iowa.

Wetterer, Margaret K. *Kate Shelley and the Midnight Express.* Minneapolis: Carolrhoda Books, Inc., 1990. Based on a true story, this book tells how an Iowa girl saved an express train from disaster.

WEBSITES

Iowa State Government Home Page
<http://www.state.ia.us/>
The state's official website contains information about state
government, education, travel, community resources, and more,
with links to other state resources.

Official Iowa Tourism Home Page
<http://www.traveliowa.com/>
This site provides resources for visitors to Iowa, including a
calendar of events; information about attractions, recreation,
and lodging; and other helpful materials for travelers.

Des Moines Register
<http://www.desmoinesregister.com>
Iowa's most famous newspaper covers news from Des Moines and
beyond, with sections on news, sports, entertainment, and more.
The paper also sponsors the famous Register's Annual Great
Bicycle Ride Across Iowa (RAGBRAI).

State Historical Society of Iowa
<http://www.iowahistory.org/>
This site contains information on the society's programs and
projects, including publications, historic preservation work,
museum exhibits, library services, and historic sites.

PRONUNCIATION GUIDE

Beiderbecke, Bix (BYE-dur-behk, BIHKS)

Corydon (KAWR-uh-duhn)

Decorah (dih-KOHR-uh)

Des Moines (dih MOYN)

Dubuque (duh-BYOOK)

Jolliet, Louis (JOH-lee-eht, LOO-his)

La Salle, Sieur de (luh SAL, syu duh)

Marquette, Jacques (mahr-KEHT, ZHAHK)

Mesquakie (muhs-KWAW-kee)

Okoboji (oh-kuh-BOH-jee)

Osage (oh-SAYJ)

GLOSSARY

crop rotation: alternating crops from one year to the next. This process helps restore nutrients to the soil.

drift: a mixture of clay, sand, gravel, and boulders deposited by a glacier, plus materials deposited by the running water of a melting glacier. Areas covered by drift have very good soil for farming.

fertilizer: a natural or artificial substance that enriches the soil, helping to produce more crops

glacier: a large body of ice and snow that moves slowly over land

groundwater: water that lies beneath the earth's surface. The water comes from rain and melting snow that seep through soil and between cracks in rocks.

herbicide: chemicals used to destroy unwanted plants such as weeds

ice age: a period when ice sheets cover large regions of the earth. The most recent ice age, called the Pleistocene, began almost 2 million years ago and ended about 10,000 years ago.

insecticide: a substance that kills insects

prairie: a large area of level or gently rolling grassy land with few trees

reservation: public land set aside by the government to be used by Native Americans

till: a mixture of clay, sand, gravel, and boulders deposited by a glacier

INDEX

PHOTO ACKNOWLEDGMENTS

Cover Photographs by © David Muench/CORBIS (left), © Craig Aumess/CORBIS (right); PresentationMaps.com, pp. 1, 8, 9, 49; © Michael S. Lewis/CORBIS, pp. 2–3; © Tom Bean/CORBIS, pp. 3, 4 (detail), 7 (detail), 18 (detail), 40 (detail), 52 (detail); © Phil Schermeister/CORBIS, p. 6; Lynda Richards, pp. 7, 13, 18, 35, 41, 43 (right), 44, 53, 58, 60, 80; © James Blank/Root Resources, p. 10; © Kent and Donna Dannen, pp. 11, 14, 40; © Ty Smedes, pp. 15 (bottom), 16, 17, 21, 59; Lucille Sukalo, p. 15 (top); © Gianni Dagli Orti/CORBIS, p. 19; State Historical Society of Iowa – Iowa City, pp. 20, 22, 25, 31, 37; Independent Picture Service, pp. 23, 69 (second from bottom); National Archives Canada,(C-8486189) detail, p. 24; National Collection of Fine Arts, Smithsonian Institution, p. 27; © Kay Shaw, pp. 27, 36, 51; © CORBIS, p. 29; State Historical Society of Iowa—Des Moines, pp. 30, 32, 34; © JeffGreenberg@juno.com, pp. 33, 54 (top); © Root Resources, p. 39; Steve Pope Photography, p. 42; Orange City Chamber & Tulip Festival Steering Committee, p. 43 (left); Photo by photographer Harry Baumert, © 2000, The Des Moines Register and Tribune Company. Reprinted with permission. p. 45; © Tom Till, p. 46; Colleen Sexton, pp. 47, 57; Oscar Mayer Foods Corporation, p. 48 (bottom right); JOLLY TIME Pop Corn, pp. 48 (top left), 56; USDA—Soil Conservation Service, p. 55; Ken Ostlie, University of Minnesota—Department of Entomology, p. 54 (bottom); Jack Lindstrom, p. 61; Halston for Men, p. 67 (second from bottom); Hollywood Book and Poster Co., p. 68 (second from top, second from bottom); Circus World Museum, Baraboo, Wisconsin, p. 69 (top); © Rune Hellestad/CORBIS, p. 66 (top); © Douglas Kirkland/CORBIS, p. 66 (second from top); Library of Congress, p. 66 (bottom); © Bettmann/CORBIS, pp. 67 (second from top), 69 (second from top), 69 (bottom); U.S. Government Printing Office, p. 67 (bottom); The George Meany Memorial Archives, p. 68 (top); San Francisco 49ers, p. 66 (second from bottom); Stew Thornley, p. 67 (top); Chase Roe, Retna Ltd., p. 68 (bottom); Jean Matheny, p. 70; © George D. Lepp/CORBIS, p. 73